So-Called "Bible-Believing" People Are In Serious Error Using Translations Other Than The 1611 King James Bible!

Bible For Today
Baptist Church

Pastor D. A. Waite, Th.D., Ph.D.

THE BIBLE FOR TODAY PRESS
900 PARK AVENUE
COLLINGSWOOD, NEW JERSY 08108
U.S.A.

CHURCH PHONE:856-854-4747
BFT PHONE:856-854-4452
ORDERS: 1-800-JOHN 10:9
BFT@BibleForToday.org
www.BibleForToday.org
fax: 856-854-2464

We Use and Defend
the King James Bible

July, 2020

ISBN: 978-1-7351454-8-8

Publishing assisted by:
The Old Paths Publications, Inc.
www.theoldpathspublications.com
TOP@theoldpathspublications.com

So-Called "Bible-Believing" People Are In Serious Error Using Translations Other Than The 1611 King James Bible!

By Pastor D. A. Waite, Th.D., Ph.D.

BFT #4208

I document the reasons for these serious doctrinal errors in twenty-seven pages of documentation concerning 133 of the 356 New Testament Bible verses that contain doctrinal errors found in the Westcott and Hort Greek New Testament. They are followed by the other two Greek texts with different names, but which usually follow the words of the Westcott and Hort Greek Text.

The problem is that the new Bible translations are used by many so-called Fundamentalists or Bible-believers. They don't see any problems using the translations based upon false Greek Words that have heretical doctrines, many of which are secretly brought into these various translations.

Because of this, I believe that every Pastor, teacher, or other person who is comfortable using these other Bible versions with so many false doctrines in them should be solidly reprimanded for promoting heretical teachings. See the twenty-seven pages that follow to see the gravity of these Satanic doctrines and teachings which are found in the New Testament Greek Text that they believe in, which is the Gnostic Westcott and Hort Greek Text.

It is unknown when and where these Bible translations will insert Westcott and Hort's heretical doctrines, but, since they think they are truthful, they might insert them anywhere in their translations. Because of this, we must beware!

July 25, 2020

BFT #4208

Some Of Westcott & Hort's (W&H) Heresies In Their Greek Text Used And Endorsed By Many "So-Called Fundamentalist Churches And Schools"

From Dr. Jack Moorman's Book
Early Manuscripts, Church Fathers, and the Authorized Version
Published by the Bible For Today Baptist Church July, 2005)

This Paper Was Compiled By Pastor D. A. Waite, Th.D., Ph.D.

Information About This Paper

(1) The partial quotations are from Dr. Moorman's book. (2) The bold and underlined words have all been omitted by the Gnostic heretics, Westcott and Hort (W&H). In their Greek New Testament, Westcott and Hort (W&H) have followed the changes of these Gnostic heretics because they agreed that these Greek words do not belong in the Greek New Testament. (3) The partial surrounding words which they have kept, are those from the Westcott and Hort (W&H) Greek text as well.

Verses from Matthew

1.   Mt. 1:25 "Brought forth her **firstborn** son." (p. 122)

They omit calling Jesus, Mary's Son, her **firstborn** Son, thus questioning His virgin birth.

2.   Mt. 8:29 "**Jesus**, thou Son of God." (p. 127)

They deny that "**Jesus**" is the "Son of God."

3.   Mt. 12:6 "That in this place is **one** greater than the temple." (p. 128)

They deny that **Jesus is "greater than the temple**."

4.   Mt. 12:25 "And **Jesus** knew their thoughts." (p. 129)

They deny that "**Jesus**" had the Divine attribute of omniscience and knew everything, including people's thoughts.

5.   Mt. 13:51 "They say unto him, Yea, **Lord**." (p. 131)

They deny the Deity of Jesus, refusing to call Him "**Lord**."

6.   Mt. 14:25 "**Jesus** went unto them, walking on the sea." (p. 132)

They deny that "**Jesus**" was Deity, and was able to "walk on the sea."

7.   Mt. 16:20 "Then charged he his disciples that they should tell no man
that he was **Jesus** the Christ." (p. 134)

W&H concluding heresy: They deny the Deity of "**Jesus**" by refusing to call Him "Christ."

8.   Mt. 18:11 "**For the son of man is come to save that which was lost**." (p. 135)

W&H concluding heresy: They deny the reason the Lord Jesus Christ came into the world. It was so that those who trust Him might be saved, because they removed from this verse: "**For the son of man is come to save that which was lost.**"

9.   Mt. 19:9 "And shall marry another, committeth adultery: **and whoso marrieth her which is put away doth commit adultery**." (p. 137)

W&H concluding heresy: They deny that those who marry those who are divorced, commit adultery.

10.   Mt. 19:17 [The Lord Jesus Christ is asking this question.] "**Why callest thou me good? There is none good but one, that is, God**." (p. 139)

W&H concluding heresy: They deny that Jesus is God, so they remove all these words.

11.   Mt. 23:8 "But be not ye called Rabbi: for one is your Master, **even Christ**; and all ye are brethren." (p. 142)

W&H concluding heresy: They deny the Deity of "**Christ**" and that He is the "Master."

12.   Mt. 24:48 "That evil servant shall say in his heart, My lord delayeth "**his coming**." (p. 144)

W&H concluding heresy: They deny "**his coming**," the 2nd coming of Christ.

13.   Mt. 25:13 "Ye know neither the day nor the hour **wherein the Son of man cometh**." (p. 145)

W&H concluding heresy: They deny the 2nd coming of the Lord Jesus Christ.

14.   Mt. 28:6 "Come, see the place where the **Lord** lay." (p. 148)

W&H concluding heresy: They deny the Deity of Christ because they refuse to believe that the bodily resurrected Saviour "**Lord**" formerly lay there in that tomb, and that He was and is "**Lord**" which they removed.

Verses from Mark

15.   Mk. 1:1 "The beginning of the gospel of Jesus Christ, **the Son of God**." (p. 149)

W&H concluding heresy: By their omission, they deny that Jesus Christ is "**the Son of God**."

16.   Mk. 3:29 "Hath never forgiveness, but is in danger of eternal **damnation**." (p. 152)

W&H concluding heresy: By removing "**damnation**," they deny there is any place for eternal "**damnation**" such as Hell.

17.   Mk.   6:34 "And **Jesus** when he came out." (p. 155)

W&H concluding heresy: They deny that the **feeding of the 5,000 occurred before** "**Jesus**" came out, so it denies that "**Jesus**" fed the 5,000.

18.   Mk. 8:1 "Having nothing to eat, **Jesus** called his disciples." (p. 156)

W&H concluding heresy: They deny that "**Jesus**" fed the 4,000.

19.   Mk. 8:17 "And when **Jesus** knew it." (p. 156)

W&H concluding heresy: They deny the Divine omniscience of the Lord "**Jesus**" Christ. Because of this, they deny that "**Jesus**" knew everything.

20.   Mk. 9:24 "**Lord**, I believe." (p. 157)

W&H concluding heresy: They deny the Deity of the Lord Jesus Christ by removing this person calling Jesus "**Lord**."

21.   Mk. 9:42 "And whosoever shall offend one of these little ones that believe **in me**." (p. 158)

W&H concluding heresy: They omit "**in me**" which questions that the Lord Jesus Christ is Someone to genuinely believe in, in order to receive eternal life.

22.   Mk. 9:46 "**Where their worm dieth not, and the fire is not quenched**." (p. 159)

W&H concluding heresy: They remove all of verse 46, therefore denying that there is "**fire**" in Hell that cannot be quenched.

23. Mk. 11:14 "And **Jesus** answered and said unto it." (p. 162)

W&H concluding heresy: They remove that "**Jesus**" answered and cursed this fig tree.

24. Mk. 11:15 "And **Jesus** went into the temple." (p. 163)

W&H concluding heresy: They remove "**Jesus**" from the temple thus denying He had just cleansed it.

25. Mk. 16:9-20 [["**Now when Jesus was risen . . . confirming the word with signs following. Amen**."]] (p. 170) All verses in double [[ ]] are omitted.

W&H concluding heresy: They remove these Words "**when Jesus was risen**" thus denying **Jesus**' bodily resurrection.

Verses from Luke

26. Lk.4:4 "It is written, That man shall not live by bread alone, **but by   every word of God**." (p. 175)

W&H concluding heresy: They deny the importance of living "**by every word of God**."

27. Lk. 4:41 "And devils . . . saying Thou art **Christ** the Son of God." (p. 176)

W&H concluding heresy: They deny that the "devils" know that "**Christ**" is Deity and is the "Son of God."

28.   Lk. 9:35 "This is my **beloved** Son." (p. 178)

W&H concluding heresy: They deny the Deity of Christ by not being God's "**beloved**" Son.

29.   Lk. 9:43 "They were all amazed . . . at all things which **Jesus** did." (p. 178)

W&H concluding heresy: They deny that it was "**Jesus**" Who did many miracles.

30.   Lk. 9:56 "**For the Son of man is not come to destroy men's lives, but to save them**. And they went to another village." (p. 179)

W&H concluding heresy: They remove that Jesus came as the "**Son of man**" "**to save**" men's lives.

31.   Lk. 9:57 "**Lord**, I will follow thee withersoever thou goest." (p. 180)

W&H concluding heresy: By removing "**Lord**," they deny that Jesus is "**Lord**"
or Deity.

32.   Lk. 9:59 "**Lord**, suffer me first." (p. 180)

W&H concluding heresy: They deny the Deity of Christ by removing "**Lord**,"
when addressing Him.

33.   Lk. 10:21 "**Jesus** rejoiced . . . I thank thee, O Father." (p. 181)

W&H concluding heresy: They eliminate "**Jesus**," thus denying His Deity.

34.   Lk.11:2a "When ye pray, say, Our Father **which art in heaven**." (p. 182)

W&H concluding heresy: They remove and thus deny that there is such a place as "**Heaven**" or that God the Father is "**in Heaven**."

35.   Lk. 22:43-44 "**And there appeared an angel unto him from heaven, strengthening him. And being in an agony he prayed more earnestly: and his sweat was as it were great drops of blood falling down to the ground**." (p. 191)

W&H concluding heresy: By removing these words, they deny "**angels**," "**heaven**," and many other words and that Jesus was in agony.

36.   Lk. 23:34 "**Then said Jesus, Father, forgive them; for they know not what they do.**" (p. 193)

W&H concluding heresy: They deny that "**Jesus**" could ask His "**Father**" to forgive people, and that He could pray to His "**Father**."

37.   Lk. 23:42 "And he said unto Jesus, **Lord**, remember me." (p. 195)

W&H concluding heresy: They deny that the Lord Jesus Christ is "**Lord**" or Deity.

38.   Lk. 24:6 "**He is not here, but is risen**." (p. 197)

W&H concluding heresy: By omitting these words, they deny that the Lord Jesus Christ was bodily "**risen**" and raised from the dead.

39.   Lk. 24:12 "**Then arose Peter, and ran unto the sepulchre; and stooping down, he beheld the linen clothes laid by themselves, and departed, wondering in himself at that which was come to pass**." (p. 198)

W&H concluding heresy: They totally omit that Jesus' clothes were in His sepulchre, and that He had been bodily resurrected from the dead.

40.   Lk. 24:36a "**Jesus** himself stood in the midst of them." (p. 198)

W&H concluding heresy: They deny that "**Jesus**" stood in the midst of His disciples, in the Upper Room, in His resurrected body, and was alive.

41.   Lk. 24:40 "**And when he had thus spoken, he shewed them his hands and his feet**." (p. 199)

W&H concluding heresy: They did not believe in Christ's bodily resurrection so they denied that Jesus could show His disciples His resurrected body's "**hands**" and "**feet**."

42.   Lk. 24:46 "Thus it is written, **and thus it behooved** Christ to suffer." (p. 200)

W&H concluding heresy: They didn't believe it "**behooved**" Christ to suffer on the cross as a sacrifice for the sins of the world.

43.   Lk. 24:51 "**And carried up into heaven**." (p. 201)

W&H concluding heresy: By omitting "**carried up into heaven**" they deny that there is a "**heaven**," and that the Lord Jesus Christ was "**carried up**" there in His resurrected body.

44.   Lk. 24:52 "And they **worshipped him**." (p. 201)

W&H concluding heresy: They deny that **Jesus** can be "**worshipped**" because they deny He is God the Son and Deity.

Verses from John

45.   John 1:18 "No man hath seen God at any time; the only begotten **Son**, which is in the bosom of the Father, he hath declared him." (p. 202)

W&H concluding heresy: They deny that Jesus Christ is God's only begotten "**Son**" and therefore, they deny His Deity.

46.   John 3:15 "That whosoever believeth in him **should not perish**, but have eternal life." (p. 205)

W&H concluding heresy: They omit "**should not perish**," thus denying there is a Hell, and that those who reject the Lord Jesus Christ as their Saviour "**perish**" in Hell for ever.

47.   John 4:42 "And know that this is indeed **the Christ**, the Saviour of the world." (p. 205)

W&H concluding heresy: They deny that "**the Christ**" is the "**Saviour of the world**" and Deity.

48. John 5:17 "But **<u>Jesus</u>** answered them, My Father worketh hitherto, and I work." (p. 207)

W&H concluding heresy: They remove "**<u>Jesus</u>**" denying that God is His Father and that they work together jointly.

49. John 6:14 "When they had seen the miracle that **<u>Jesus</u>** did." (p. 209)

W&H concluding heresy: They deny that "**<u>Jesus</u>**" performed this "**miracle**," thus denying His Deity.

50. John 6:39 "And this is the **<u>Father's</u>** will which hath sent me." (p. 209)

W&H concluding heresy: They deny that the "**<u>Father</u>**" sent Christ into the world, thus denying His Deity.

51. John 6:47 "Verily, verily, I say unto you, he that believeth **<u>on me</u>** hath everlasting life." (p. 210)

W&H concluding heresy: They deny that believing "**<u>on me</u>**" [the Lord Jesus Christ] **is needed to receive "everlasting life**." This is a very serious heresy that many versions have used.

52. John 6:65 "Except it were given unto him of **<u>my</u>** Father." (p. 210)

W&H concluding heresy: They deny that God is the Father of the Lord Jesus Christ, thus denying His Deity.

53.   John 6:69 "**That Christ, the Son of the living God**." (p. 211)
W&H concluding heresy: They deny that "**Christ**" is "**the Son of the living God**," thus denying His Deity and being a Member of the Trinity.

54.   John 7:8 "I go not up **yet** unto this feast." (p. 211)
W&H concluding heresy: By removing "**yet**" it makes Christ a liar because He **did** go up to Jerusalem.

55.   John 8:28 "I do nothing of myself; but as **my** Father hath taught me, I speak these things." (p. 213)
W&H concluding heresy: They remove "**my**" showing that Christ is not Deity or the Son of the Father.

56.   John 8:29 "And he that sent me is with me: the **Father** hath not left me alone." (p. 213)
W&H concluding heresy: They do not state that God is Christ's "**Father**" thus denying His Deity.

57.   John 8:38 "I speak that which I have seen with **my** Father: and ye do that which ye have seen with your father." (p. 214)
W&H concluding heresy: They drop out "**my**" before "**Father**" which denies His Deity and that God is His Father.

58. John 8:59 "But Jesus hid himself, and went out of the temple, **going through the midst of them**, and so passed by." (p. 214)

W&H concluding heresy: They deny that the Lord Jesus Christ went right through the crowd that wanted to murder Him because they didn't believe He could do it, yet, He did it, as His Deity had God's power to do this, being God the Son.

59. John 9:35 "Dost thou believe on the Son **of God**"? (p. 215)

W&H concluding heresy: They omit "**of God**" because they deny that Jesus is the Son of God and Deity.

60. John 9:38-39 "**And he said, Lord, I believe. And he worshipped him**." (p.   216)

W&H concluding heresy: They omit all these words, and by omitting "**he worshipped Him**" it shows they did not believe Jesus is God and should be worshipped.

61. John 10:29 "My Father, **which** gave them me, is greater than all." (p. 216)

W&H concluding heresy: They remove "**which**" because it closely unites God the Father and God the Son, which they oppose.

62. John 10:32 "Many good works have I shewed you from **my** Father." (p. 217)

W&H concluding heresy: They remove "**my**" because they deny that God the Father is indeed the Lord Jesus Christ's Father.

63.   John 13:3 "**Jesus**" knowing that the Father had given all things into his hands." (p. 217)

W&H concluding heresy: They remove "**Jesus**" because they deny His omniscience and His closeness to His Father.

64.   John 14:17 "For he dwelleth with you, and **shall be** in you." (p. 218)

W&H concluding heresy: They remove "**shall be**" because they deny Christ is for ever, and genuine Christians shall be for ever with Christ.

65.   John 14:28 "I go unto the Father: for **my** Father is greater than I." (p. 219)

W&H concluding heresy: They deny that the Father is Jesus' eternal Father Who is with Christ, part of the eternal Trinity.

66.   John 16:10 "Of righteousness, because I go to **my** Father." (p. 219)

W&H concluding heresy: They deny that Jesus is the Son of God the Father, thus denying His joint-Deity with God the Father.

67.   John 17:17 "Sanctify them through **thy** truth." (p. 221)

W&H concluding heresy: They deny that Christ is any part of "**thy**" truth, which are the Words of the Bible.

68.   John 19:26 "He saith unto **his** mother, Woman, behold thy son!" (p. 222)

W&H concluding heresy: They deny that Mary was **His** virgin mother.

69.   John 20:17 "For I am not yet ascended to **my** Father." (p. 223)

W&H concluding heresy: They deny the Deity of Christ by removing His relationship with His eternal "Father."

Verses from Acts

70.   Acts 2:30 "That of the fruit of his loins, **according to the flesh, he would raise up Christ** to sit on his throne." (p. 224)

W&H concluding heresy: They deny Christ's bodily resurrection.

71.   Acts 3:26 "God, having raised up his Son **Jesus**, sent him to bless you." (p. 225)

W&H concluding heresy: They deny that "**Jesus**" is God's Son, thus denying His Deity.

72.   Acts 8:37 "**And Philip said, If thou believest with all thine heart, thou mayest. And he answered and said, I believe that Jesus Christ is the Son of God**." (p. 228)

W&H concluding heresy: They deny "**that Jesus Christ is the Son of God**."

73.   Acts 9:29 "He spake boldly in the name of the Lord **Jesus**." (p. 229)

W&H concluding heresy: By removing "**Jesus**," they deny the Deity of the Lord Jesus.

74.   Acts 15:11 "Through the grace of the Lord Jesus **Christ** we shall be saved." (p. 231)

W&H concluding heresy: They deny that the "Lord Jesus" is "**Christ**," and therefore is not Deity.

75.   Acts 16:31 "Believe on the Lord Jesus **Christ,** and thou shalt be saved." (p. 232)

W&H concluding heresy: They deny that believing on "**Christ**" is necessary to be "**saved**" and deny that the Lord Jesus "**Christ**" is Deity.

76.   Acts 19:4 "That they should believe on him which should come after him, that is, on **Christ** Jesus." (p. 233)

W&H concluding heresy: They believe that Jesus is not part of "**Christ**" and therefore not Deity.

77.   Acts 19:10 "All . . . heard the word of the Lord **Jesus**." (p. 233)

W&H concluding heresy: They don't believe "**Jesus**" is "Lord" therefore He is not Deity.

78.   Acts 20:21 "Repentance toward God, and faith toward our Lord Jesus   **Christ**." (p. 234)

W&H concluding heresy: They remove Lord Jesus from "**Christ**" thus removing His Deity.

Verses from Romans

79.   Romans 1:16 "For I am not ashamed of the gospel **of Christ**." (p. 237)

W&H concluding heresy: They remove "**of Christ**" from the gospel which fails to identify which gospel it is.

80.   Romans 5:1 "Therefore being justified by faith, **we have** peace with God." (p. 237)

W&H concluding heresy: They fail to affirm that those who are justified by true faith in Christ, immediately have peace with God."

81.   Romans 6:11 "Alive unto God through Jesus Christ **our Lord**." (p. 238)

W&H concluding heresy: They deny that Jesus Christ is "**Lord**" thus denying His Deity.

82.   Romans 13:9 "Thou shalt not steal, **Thou shalt not bear false witness**, Thou shalt not covet." (p. 241)

W&H concluding heresy: They do not believe that "**Thou shalt not bear false witness**" is true so they can lie all the time as they continually do.

83.   Romans 14:10 "For we shall all stand before the judgment seat **of Christ**." (p. 241)

W&H concluding heresy: They deny there will ever be a judgment seat "**of Christ**" where all genuine Christians will be judged by the Lord Jesus Christ Himself.

84.   Romans 15:8 "Now I say that **Jesus** Christ was a minister of the circumcision." (p. 242)
W&H concluding heresy: They deny that "**Jesus**" was a "minister of the circumcision" and since He is not connected with "Christ," they deny His Deity.

85.   Romans 16:18 "For they that are such serve not our Lord **Jesus** Christ." (p. 243)
W&H concluding heresy: Since they remove "**Jesus**" from "Lord" and "Christ," they deny His Deity.

86.   Romans 16:20 "The grace of our Lord Jesus **Christ** be with you." (p. 244) **W&H concluding heresy:** Since they remove "Jesus" from "**Christ**," they deny His Deity.

Verses from 1 Corinthians

87.   1 Corinthians 5:4a "In the name of our Lord Jesus **Christ**." (p. 244)
W&H concluding heresy: They remove "Jesus" from "**Christ**" thus denying His Deity.

88.   1 Corinthians 5:4b "With the power of our Lord Jesus **Christ**." (p. 245)
W&H concluding heresy: They remove "Jesus" from "**Christ**," they again deny His Deity.

89.   1 Corinthians 5:5 "That the spirit may be saved in the day of the Lord **Jesus**." (p. 245)
W&H concluding heresy: Since they remove "**Jesus**" from "Lord" they deny His Deity.

90.   1 Corinthians 5:7 Christ . . . is sacrificed **for us**."
(p. 246)
W&H concluding heresy: They deny Christ's death
was "**for us**" meaning in place of everyone who ever
lived, thus denying His substitutionary atonement for
the sins of the world.

91.   1 Corinthians 6:20 "Glorify God in your body,
and in your spirit, which are God's." (p. 246)
W&H concluding heresy: They deny that true
Christians' bodies and "**spirit**" "**are God's**."

92.   1 Corinthians 9:1 "Have I not seen Jesus **Christ**
our Lord"? (p. 248)
W&H concluding heresy: Since they remove "Jesus"
from "**Christ**," they deny His Deity.

Verses from 2 Corinthians

93.   2 Corinthians 4:14 "Shall raise up us also **by**
Jesus." (p. 255)
W&H concluding heresy: They deny the power of
"Jesus" to raise up genuine Christians from the dead,
thus denying His Deity.

94.   2 Corinthians 5:18 "Who hath reconciled us to
himself by **Jesus** Christ." (p. 256)
W&H concluding heresy: They deny that God has
reconciled genuine Christians to Himself by "**Jesus**."

95.   2 Corinthians 11:31 "The God and Father of our Lord Jesus **Christ**."   (p. 257)

W&H concluding heresy: They teach that God is not the "God and Father" of our "Lord Jesus **Christ**."

Verses from Galatians

96.   Galatians 3:17 "The covenant, that was confirmed before of God **in Christ**." (p. 258)

W&H concluding heresy: They remove "**in Christ**" thus denying that Christ confirmed redemption's covenant. This denies His Deity.

97.   Galatians 4:7 "And if a son, then an heir of God **through Christ**. (p. 259)

W&H concluding heresy: They deny that a true Christian is an heir of God "**through Christ**," thus teaching blatant heresy!

98.   Galatians 6:15 "For **in Christ Jesus** neither circumcision availeth anything, or uncircumcision." (p. 260)

W&H concluding heresy: They falsely teach that being "**in Christ Jesus**" has no effect on circumcision or uncircumcision.

Verses from Ephesians

99.   Ephesians 3:9 "God, who created all things **by Jesus Christ**." (p. 262)
W&H concluding heresy: They deny that "**by Jesus Christ**" God created all things, thus denying His Deity and Creative Power.

100. Ephesians 3:14 "For this cause I bow my knees unto the Father **of our Lord Jesus Christ**." (p. 262)
W&H concluding heresy: They teach the heresy that God is not the Father of "**our Lord Jesus Christ**."

Verses from Philippians

101. Philippians 4:13 "I can do all things through **Christ** which strengtheneth me." (p. 265)
W&H concluding heresy: They deny the power of "**Christ**" to strengthen Paul or any other true Christian, making "**Christ**" powerless rather than omnipotent. This takes away Christ's power to help those He has redeemed.

Verses from Colossians

102. Colossians 1:2 "Peace, from God our Father and **the Lord Jesus Christ**." (p. 265)
W&H concluding heresy: They deny that peace also can come from "**the Lord Jesus Christ**," thus questioning His Deity.

103. Colossians 1:28 "That we may present every man perfect in Christ **Jesus**." (p. 266)

W&H concluding heresy: They remove "**Jesus**" from Christ, thus denying His Deity.

Verses from 1 Thessalonians

104. 1Thessalonians 1:1 "Grace be unto you, and peace, **from God the Father, and the Lord Jesus Christ**." (p. 268)

W&H concluding heresy: They remove that grace and peace might be given "**from God the Father, and the Lord Jesus Christ**" thus denying Their power and Deity.

105. 1 Thessalonians 3:11 "Now God himself and our Father, and our Lord Jesus **Christ**, direct our way unto you." (p. 269)

W&H concluding heresy: They remove the "Lord Jesus" from being "**Christ**," thus removing Him from His Deity.

106. 1 Thessalonians 3:13 "At the coming of our Lord Jesus **Christ**." (p. 270)

W&H concluding heresy: They deny that Jesus is "**Christ**" thus denying His Deity and His 2nd Coming.

Verses from 1 Timothy

107. 1 Timothy 1:1 "By the commandment of God our Saviour and **Lord** Jesus Christ." (p. 272)
W&H concluding heresy: By removing "**Lord**," they deny that Jesus Christ is "**Lord**," thus denying His Deity.

108. 1 Timothy 2:7 "I speak the truth **in Christ**." (p. 273)
W&H concluding heresy: They, by removing "**Christ**" from the truth, deny He is the "truth" and, as Deity, He supports the truth.

109. 1 Timothy 3:16 "Great is the mystery of godliness: **God** was manifest in the flesh." (p. 273)
W&H concluding heresy: They remove "**God**" from being manifested in the flesh, thus denying that the Lord Jesus Christ is "**God**" and Deity.

110. 1 Timothy 5:21 "I charge thee before God, and the **Lord** Jesus Christ, and the elect angels." (p. 276)
W&H concluding heresy: They remove "**Lord**" from "Jesus Christ" thus denying His Deity.

111. 1 Timothy 6:19 "That they may lay hold **on eternal life**." (p. 278)
W&H concluding heresy: They remove "**on eternal life**" being possible to hold on to in this life which is heretical.

Verses from 2 Timothy

112. 2 Timothy 2:19 "Let everyone that nameth the name of **Christ**." (p. 279)
W&H concluding heresy: They remove "**Christ**" Who is Deity and the Son of God.

113. 2 Timothy 4:1a "Before God, and the **Lord** Jesus Christ." (p. 279)
W&H concluding heresy: They remove "**Lord**" from Jesus Christ, thus denying His Deity.

114. 2 Timothy 4:1b "Jesus Christ, who shall judge the quick and the dead **at** his appearing." (p. 280)
W&H concluding heresy: They remove "**at**" which is the time Christ will appear thus denying that Christ will return to this earth again.

115. 2 Timothy 4:22 "The Lord **Jesus Christ** be with thy spirit." (p. 280)
W&H concluding heresy: They separate "Lord" from "**Jesus Christ**" thus removing His Deity.

Verses from Titus

116. Titus 1:4 "From God the Father and the **Lord** Jesus Christ our Saviour." (p. 281)
W&H concluding heresy: They remove "**Lord**" from "Jesus Christ" thus denying His Deity.

Verses from Hebrews

117. Hebrews 1:3 "When he had **by himself** purged our sins." (p. 281)

W&H concluding heresy: They remove that the Lord Jesus Christ "**by himself**" on the cross died for the sins of the world, so that those who trust Him might be cleansed and have eternal life.

118. Hebrews 3:1 "Consider the Apostle and High Priest of our profession, **Christ** Jesus." (p. 282)

W&H concluding heresy: They remove "**Christ**" from Jesus, thus denying His Deity.

119. Hebrews 10:34 "Knowing in yourselves that ye have **in heaven** a better and an enduring substance." (p. 285)

W&H concluding heresy: They deny that there is a literal place "**in heaven**."

Verses from 1 Peter

120. 1 Peter 2:24 "By **whose** stripes ye were healed." (p. 288)

W&H concluding heresy: They deny that by "**whose**" stripes and wounds on the cross people were healed spiritually. They deny Christ's substitutionary atonement on the cross, dying for the sins of the world. This is heresy!

121. 1 Peter 4:1 "Forasmuch then as Christ hath suffered **for us** in the flesh." (p. 289)
W&H concluding heresy: They deny Christ's provisionary substitutionary atonement on the cross for the sins of the entire world.

122. 1 Peter 5:10 "Who hath called us unto his eternal glory by Christ **Jesus**." (p. 291)
W&H concluding heresy: They deny that "**Jesus**" is Christ, thus denying His Deity.

Verses from 2 Peter

123. 2 Peter 2:17 ". . . darkness is reserved **for ever**." (p. 293)
W&H concluding heresy: They deny that Hell is . . . darkness lasting "**for ever**."

Verses from 1 John

124. 1 John 1:7 "And the blood of Jesus **Christ** his Son." (p. 295)
W&H concluding heresy: They deny Jesus' Deity and question the efficacy of His Blood by removing Jesus from "**Christ**."

125. 1 John 2:28 "**When** he shall appear." (p. 297)
W&H concluding heresy: They remove "**when**" thus denying the second coming of Christ.

126. 1 John 5:13 "That ye may know that ye have eternal life, **and that ye may believe on the name of the Son of God**." (p. 300)

W&H concluding heresy: They remove "**believe on the name of the Son of God**," and thus deny that Jesus is the "**Son of God**" and that that belief will give them "eternal life."

Verses from 2 John

127. 2 John 3 "From God the Father, and from **the Lord** Jesus Christ."   (p. 300)

W&H concluding heresy: They remove the Deity of Jesus Christ by removing "**Lord**" in front of Jesus Christ.

128. 2 John 9b "He that abideth in the doctrine **of Christ**, he hath both the Father and the Son." (p. 301)

W&H concluding heresy: They remove "**Christ**" being the source of proper doctrine.

Verses from Revelation

129. Revelation 1:9a "And in the kingdom and patience of Jesus **Christ**." (p. 303)

W&H concluding heresy: They remove the Deity of "Jesus" by removing Him from being "**Christ**."

130. Revelation 11:17 "Which art, and wast, **and art to come**." (p. 306)

W&H concluding heresy: They deny Christ's 2nd coming by removing "**art to come**."

131. Revelation 16:5b "Which art, and wast, **and shalt be**." (p. 308)

W&H concluding heresy: They deny the second coming of the Lord Jesus Christ by removing "**and shalt be**."

132. Revelation 21:24 "And the nations **of them which are saved** shall walk in the light of it." (p. 311)

W&H concluding heresy: They deny that **only** the saved true Christians among the nations shall walk in the light.

133. Revelation 22:21 "The grace of our Lord Jesus **Christ**." (p. 312)

W&H concluding heresy: They deny the Deity of Jesus by removing "**Christ**."

BFT #4208

For extra copies, Check the Cost, Shipping, & Handling, by Calling Bible For Today at 856-261-9018

www.ingramcontent.com/pod-product-compliance
Lightning Source LLC
Chambersburg PA
CBHW051051030426
42339CB00006B/297